The Birthday of a King

Written *by* Bob Hartman
Illustrated *by* Michael McGuire

For Mom and Dad and all those Christmas mornings. B.H.

To Rosie with love for her strength and support. M.M.

VICTOR BOOKS
A Division of Scripture Press Publications Inc.

What do you do for the birthday of a King?
You have a parade, that's what.
With flowery floats, and marching bands, and giant bouncing balloons.
Jesus was a King.
And there was a parade for His birthday too.

A long walk from Nazareth up north,
     to Bethlehem down south.
A caravan of people, off to pay their taxes.
Rich and poor.
Old and young.
Men and women.
And two people in particular—
     a man named Joseph,
     and Mary, his very
     pregnant wife.
What do you do for
     the birthday of a King?
You have a parade, that's what.

What do you do for the birthday of a King?
You find a special place.
A ballroom, maybe. With marble floors,
        and painted ceilings, and gold chandeliers.
Jesus was a King.
And His parents found a special place for His birthday too.

There were no ballrooms.
    And the hotel rooms were all full.
But there was an empty stable.
With a dirt floor, and a wooden roof,
    and a dangling cobweb or two.
What do you do for the birthday of a King?
You find a special place.

What do you do for the birthday of a King?
You shoot off fireworks, of course!

You fill the sky with pinwheels and daisies
and a rumbling rocket racket.
Jesus was a King.
And there were fireworks
at His birthday too.

Shooting stars, heavenly hosts, and a full piece angel band.

What do you do for the birthday of a King?

You shoot off fireworks, of course!

What do you do for the birthday of a King?

You send out invitations.

To Dukes, and Knights, and Lords and Ladies.

Very Important Guests.

Jesus was a King.

And there were invitations to His birthday too.

"You are invited," said the angel, "to a stable in the town of Bethlehem."

"You are invited!" said the angel to the shepherds and their sheep.

"You are invited," said the angel. "There will be plenty of hay for all!"

What do you do for the birthday of a King?

You send out invitations.

What do you do for the birthday of a King?

You bring presents, that's what.

Silver, shiny things.

Fun and fancy things.

No boring things like underwear or socks.

Jesus was a King.

And He got presents too.

His father's care.

His mother's love.

And a very nice set of swaddling clothes, whatever they are.

What do you do for the birthday of a King?
You bring presents, that's what.

What do you do for
    the birthday of a King?
You throw a party.
    The biggest you can.
You eat eats, and sing songs,
    and give gifts.
And every member of the royal
    family is there.

Jesus is a King.

And every year we throw a party for Him.

A party that goes right around the world!

We eat eats, and sing songs, and give gifts.

And every member of the royal family is there:

His brothers and sisters.

You and me!

What do we do for the birthday of the King?

We throw a party.
And we call it Christmas.

Other books in this series are:
The Morning of the World (the story of God's Creation)
The Edge of the River (the story of baby Moses and his sister Miriam)
The Middle of the Night (the story of young Samuel called by God)

The story you have just read is based on Luke 2:1-20 and Matthew 2:1-12.
We encourage you to read the Bible passage itself and
discover even more about God's wonderful Word.

Art direction: Paul Higdon/Grace K. Chan Mallette
Production: Myrna Hasse
Editing: Liz Morton Duckworth

ISBN: 1-56476-04043-X

1 2 3 4 5 6 7 8 9 10 Printing/Year 97 96 95 94 93

VICTOR BOOKS
A division of SP Publications, Inc.
Wheaton, Illinois 60187